I Saw the Light . . .

But No One Asked Me to Stay . . .

CYNTHIA DUSENBERY

Balboa Press books may be ordered through booksellers or by contacting:

Balboa Press
A Division of Hay House
1663 Liberty Drive
Bloomington, IN 47403
www.balboapress.com
1 (877) 407-4847

Because of the dynamic nature of the Internet, any web addresses or links contained in this book may have changed since publication and may no longer be valid. The views expressed in this work are solely those of the author and do not necessarily reflect the views of the publisher, and the publisher hereby disclaims any responsibility for them.

Any people depicted in stock imagery provided by Getty Images are models, and such images are being used for illustrative purposes only. Certain stock imagery © Getty Images.

ISBN: 978-1-9822-2456-1 (sc)
ISBN: 978-1-9822-2457-8 (e)

Library of Congress Control Number: 2019903536

Print information available on the last page.

Balboa Press rev. date: 03/27/2019

BALBOA
PRESS
A DIVISION OF HAY HOUSE

I SAW THE LIGHT….
BUT NO ONE ASKED ME TO STAY….

MY CRASH COURSE IN COMPASSION

Yes, by that title I am trying to put a playful bent on a topic that in some circles causes controversy. I sure wasn't expecting this event to happen to me, let alone writing about it. Some events in our lives we would like to stay hidden but this was one that had to be shared. And something was nudging me in that direction. For every believer in supernatural events there are at least two skeptics to chime in. That's probably why I published fiction for my first book. It's a story told in rhyme by a cartoon character. Nothing controversial there. I certainly don't look for controversy but this event plopped down in my life and I was getting more than a whisper to tell the world about it. I will share this miracle at first in segments. *So here we go…….*

People have spoken of near death experiences and speak of being drawn to a light on the horizon. Yes, I did see that beautiful heavenly destination in the distance but did not seem to be moving toward it. I guess sometimes you don't go beyond the Light or get guided to it. A determination must have been made that it was not going to be my last day on earth. In my case I was protected by The Light from the trauma, pain and more serious injuries that could have taken my life and then I was sent on my way to learn from it. For now I will give you just a little peek into the experience and go into the full and more miraculous details a bit later.

In this experience I was existing peacefully in The Light and was feeling loved and protected but did not find myself proceeding to what I saw in the distance. I surmise this was the door to Heaven or the afterlife. I did not see passed loved ones coming to greet me or guide me to that passageway. Remember that song about knocking on Heaven's door? Well I wasn't nor was I given a choice. I got the protection I needed just in the nick of time and I am grateful.

Let me start to tell you just a little about this miraculous event. I remember that fateful afternoon just walking home and suddenly being surrounded by a Light and being taken from my current reality. I was walking on the sidewalk near the flower garden by this restaurant. I was not having a medical situation of any sorts. I wasn't in a panic as to what was happening. It was peaceful and felt natural. I then saw a beautiful heavenly destination in the distance. I suddenly felt a gentle breeze wash over me and intuitively felt there was a presence with me so I questioned about that breeze. I mean I actually heard myself speak the words "What was that poof of energy?" I did not hear a response but got brought back to current reality. That return or my answer came in what felt like an instant. So that is the basic scenario without the deeper elements that made it so incredible. I know that is pretty incredible in itself, but there is more.

Let me delve into some amazing and miraculous aspects to that "gentle breeze" a bit later. The core of the miracle.

But for now I want to weave in a bit of my old life before I go into more details of the miracle. Maybe you will surmise as I did, why the journey may have been allowed to happen. The miraculous event also opened my eyes to the many aspects of Compassion: The Divine Love and Compassion from our Creator, Compassion to and from others, and also learning much needed Compassion for myself. The event opened up my eyes to a few other insights or perceptions along the way but mostly how I felt my faith or belief in the power of prayer played a role in this gift happening to me.

WAS THIS A WAKE-UP CALL?

I sure needed a wake-up call in life. I used to be a person who kept running and running on a hamster wheel. I considered myself a lively and quite healthy senior citizen. I was still running my own business although in a much smaller scale in what I called a semi-retirement. I loved the poetry of rhyme and took it upon myself to self-publish a poetry book. I did my own book promotion on social media mixed in with administrative functions of the business. So you can see my days were full. I kept ignoring the fact that I was no longer getting joy from my business and thought way too many times of closing the doors for good. I had even discussed this fact with clients and they would ask me if I could take on their work anyway if I ever closed the business. So I just kept the business running and feeling I was not getting away.

Since it was such an effort on my part starting this particular type of business, I also had those pangs of not wanting to let it go. I was just like a parent that won't let go of the child wanting to leave home and spread their wings but at the same time eyeing that new spare room opening up for an exercise room. It was hard to deal with that double whammy and I was not strong enough to come to a resolution. So I kept the business alive and plugged along. Although I never felt that way with the book project or the social media promotion and always felt so energized doing that. Was I getting a nudge from the Universe to change course? Was I listening? No, I kept running on that hamster wheel.

Now I am not saying that what is to follow was our Creator's giant nudge, but I believe the event was allowed to happen, yet with great protection and perhaps the intention of a nudge was an afterthought. I believe I had more important lessons to learn from this event and I believe the Creator was going to give me time and some space by taking me off the hamster wheel to learn them. I had to close my business office that fateful day and it remains closed and the corporation was dissolved.

So many financial issues came into my life to join a myriad of other stifling issues. As if by magic during recovery time, I found a Caroline Myss CD entitled, Defy Gravity. That CD was probably a gift or bought at an I Can Do It conference many years ago and had been shelved. The CD wrapper was never even opened but sitting among the other used CDs and found its way into my hands after release from medical facilities. In that CD she speaks of someone losing everything and having a Life Tsunami. Was that CD waiting for this moment in time? Interesting, huh? A Life Tsunami aptly described my current situation. A situation of excessive hospital bills and financial loss, a business closing, and severe injuries that were going to take a long healing period that would change my existence. The floodgate was open and the safe ground was slipping away.

But now, I think it is time to take you to that fateful day and introduce you to the whole Miracle. Some dialog may be repetitive since I presented some of the scenario before but it needs repeating.

BUCKLE UP

I was a big walker and would run my errands for household or business on foot since I did not drive. I liked it that way as burning calories left room for more fun foods to enter my refrigerator.

That fateful Friday afternoon in August 2017 had me tossing around in my head if I should do one more errand outside. Later I would think I just should have stayed home. But maybe if this situation was avoided, could something different come around again to get my attention? Not knowing the workings of the Universe I will just close the door to thinking about my decision that day anymore. What convinced me that day to run the extra errand was the fact it was such a nice cool day and perfect for a bit of walking. So I left to get to the store by a village bus and decided to do a refreshing walk back home as I had done on so many occasions.

I was walking only a short distance from my home when I started to be surrounded in a beautiful White Light taking my vision of my surroundings from me. I was not having any health issue before or while this was happening to me. I had just been walking on the sidewalk next to a restaurant's flower garden and that was my last visual. I was being swept from my earth reality. I could see in the distance a beautiful vision which looked to me like a heavenly door of sorts with an even stronger beaming light behind it. It looked like a door covered with a white shiny textured satin appearance. I remember not being frightened by what was happening and actually felt quite peaceful in this state of being. I am assuming now if I was to have died that day, I would have been travelling toward the beaming door in the distance. Perhaps then, what I thought was a door, would have opened and loved ones that passed would have greeted me to help with any adjustments.

In this beautiful state of being, I suddenly felt a gentle movement of energy almost like a soft breeze blow over me and I remember hearing myself calmly saying "What was that poof of energy?" Was I talking to God? Was I talking to a Guardian Angel? After questioning about the poof of energy, and it seemed instantly, my awareness was in the back of a parked ambulance yet still feeling no pain…no excitement…no trauma. Oh but it seems there had been. I had not felt nor seen any trauma while in The Light so I had no knowledge yet as to what happened. I remember a neighbor coming to the ambulance door stating he was taking my shopping bag home to hang on my door for my return and I calmly acknowledged that. Yes, the accident was that close to my home. But yet, there is something intriguing as to the accident site for me to discuss later.

I then tried to move my leg and questioned the paramedic why my leg would not move. The paramedic replied I was just hit by a car and he proceeded to ask if they could cut off my clothes and purse strap away from my body; apparently due to the fact they thought or could see I had many broken bones. They even cut off only one shoe as the other apparently came off on impact on the leg with several broken bones. I would later learn of a skin injury on that foot which eventually required two skin surgeries; one being a skin grafting. I needed four surgeries in all for broken bones and skin. Yet, when I was in The Light and feeling that "poof of energy" which I assume was the energy of the car hitting me, I did not feel any impact bump, bruise, broken bones, impact of slam to ground, or tearing of skin. Yet I had all that. I actually had bone injuries on my elbow on right side, and my ankle bone and knee on other side. One side I guess from impact of car and the other side after being thrown to ground in fall. Finally I learned apparently on impact and falling back I took a hit to my head when hitting the ground and got bleeding on the brain, yet never felt the pain when I got that thump on my head either. I just felt a gentle breeze like energy blow over me when protected in The Light.

My attorney told me in the driver's deposition, he related after impact I fell on my back and he could see I was in pain. Yet, I was not in pain at that time while in The Light and never felt any pain upon impact or even when my awareness was back in the ambulance. I was already protected by The Light well before impact and only felt that gentle breeze like "poof of energy".

In fact, I remember where I was walking when first surrounded by The Light. Remember I was waiting to tell you something about the accident site? I was coming upon a driveway; yet I was struck by the car at a completelydifferent driveway many, many feet away from the first driveway. Of course, this caused me confusion when I first spoke to an attorney about a lawsuit and where the accident took place. And I remained in that ignorance for many months. It was only through court documents that I saw pictures of the actual site and I was totally amazed. Was I walking quite a bit of distance to the eventual accident site while sheltered in The Light? I sure think so.

So while I was in The Light I had no idea there was an impact on my body with a vehicle, the feeling of pain or injury of broken bones and tearing skin, or where or what trauma was going on. As I said before, I only felt a breeze like poof of energy. Why was I protected from seeing and feeling the trauma? God knows best I guess and perhaps the trauma itself could have killed me by shock or heart attack. That's my insight.

Another thought…. was I purposely captured in The Light and positioned in place with the view of the heavenly home I would or could be travelling to, so I would realize death may have been on the table but I was being saved? It would help me realize all other aspects of the Miracle. Maybe I was meant to see that glorious destination in that state of being to help me understand why I had no pain or trauma while it was happening. Maybe I was meant to know this was God's connection or display.

Time seemed to be different in that state, realm or wherever being in The Light was. As I consider when and where I became enveloped by The Light and where I was eventually hit, I had walked many feet while in this state of being before impact. Yet things were happening so fast in The Light. Same as to when I questioned in The Light about the poof of energy gently blowing over me and my answer felt like it came in an instant bringing me back to my old awareness. Yet the time from impact, which I assume was the painless poof of energy, it had to be at least 15 minutes or more for calling an ambulance and arrival, and more time getting me into the ambulance. It was busy Friday afternoon traffic. So I tend to agree with those that say there is no time in the greater realms and also I guess on the path thereto.

So The Light protected me from the actual trauma and pain of the accident and for some time thereafter . I eventually went unconscious as I do not remember getting to the hospital in that ambulance, or ER functions. Thank you God for that too. There was no more interaction with The Light in that unconscious state.

I believe now that I was protected from even more serious injury as doctors, nurses and others would say upon meeting me, that I should be dead. It was then I would jokingly state for some reason "I saw The Light but no one asked me to stay." Thus, I got my book title. I realize now The Light was God. Although I do not believe God planned this accident, I believe He knew it was going to happen and protected my life, and from experiencing the pain and trauma of it. The impact must have been quite strong. I remember how I felt when I eventually got home and looked inside the purse that had been cut away from my body and saw a mirror in many broken pieces. The size and impact of that car on a little five foot, 70 year old slender senior citizen could have created way more damage. God even kept me safe from the pulmonary embolism I developed while in the hospital. And I remember I never felt the fear the medical people or my brother had upon its discovery. Probably because I had felt the protection of God and knowing what I had experienced and they did not. I guess I thought about what a miracle God had shown in the accident to keep me alive, He was not going to let a pulmonary embolism get in the way.

Like I said I did not feel the impact or any breaking of bones or tearing of skin in the process…. just the surrounding peaceful Light with a view of an even greater beaming destination in the distance, and that poof of energy. Can't say it was all because of head damage as that injury only happened in hitting the ground after the impact. I was already in The Light well before impact. God in His compassionate miracle regulated that I would not experience the trauma and pain and He regulated the injuries to be allowed. Being All Knowing, He knew what I could handle. God knows intimately all of His Creation.

Only my perspective, but in the healing process, I remember listening to a news story of a young man beaten and burned. They said he was alive when put in a garbage can to burn after the beating. My first thoughts were he probably was already taken in the protection of God when the going got rough. The thugs were seeing him in pain, but I truly wonder if he was really there or already in the Hands of God before going Home? Remember the driver that hit me said upon impact he saw me in pain when on the ground but I was still surrounded in God's protection at that time. Remember The Light surrounded me a bit of a distance from where I actually got hit and I must have looked to the public like I was normally walking along, but I was already surrounded in God's protection. After the hit I looked to others as if I was in pain. I don't think God just showed me special treatment. Perhaps all His children are taken into protection during trauma events long before they start the journey to The Light to go home. I was taken off that ultimate journey. I don't have definite knowledge this happens just what I feel after what happened to me and I believe in a God of Compassion for all His children.

God had showered me with a great gift of His compassion and just let me transition not to death but to a new life.

DID BELIEF PLAY A ROLE?

It took several weeks of reviewing the event in my head but eventually I gave myself permission to accept that I had actually experienced God's protection which I had prayed for daily. I guess He did hear my protection prayers after all.

All God's children are special in His eyes and what was done for me I assume could happen to anyone. But maybe I secured my protection that day with my belief in my protection prayer. I actually made a request to God daily in deep belief I was being heard and then protected.

I walked that sidewalk along the busy road where I was hit all the time as the cars zoomed by. I never had a fear of walking along that road, which was more like a highway, because I really believed in my protection prayer. Oddly, that main road was not the culprit that day as the driver was on a driveway leading to it. My vulnerability had always been with those side streets or driveways for years as I had a few incidents with drivers trying to get on that main road. But God had heard my daily general protection prayer and this was His time to show it. Now you may think, so what kind of protection did I get because I did get hit after all? But I was saved from the pain and trauma in the Miracle and I did not die when I truly should have. So I consider that huge protection.

All this is just my insight, but I have heard how belief is key in the power of prayer. I would say a particular prayer each morning asking for God and the Angels to protect me on my journey each day. Funny I had a close call years before involving another driver coming out of a different driveway trying to get on that same main road and thus, why I developed that vulnerability. So it was about then that I started to ask daily for some intervention or Divine help. Interesting, huh?

I do this same kind of protection prayer for my home every night as I would shut things down before bed. I remember thinking one day if a tornado should hit this condo building I bet there would be windows blown out everywhere but no damage to this condo unit! Yes I may have said that jokingly but my belief was that strong. So not only did I learn of God's love and compassion, I think I may have also gotten proof of the power of belief and faith in prayer. The Creator wants to help us with this life journey if we only ask. I look back now at my saying that daily prayer and I do remember that it was not just a mumbling of words but I truly felt I was speaking to God and I was going to get God's protection. And I sure did! Guess saying it for a few years set the belief deep inside me.

This is my perception. I am hardly the person to preach to the choir but I have seen a few other beliefs work their magic in my life. I won't go into them as this is not a book on belief. But I would be remiss if I did not state that since the miracle that fateful day, I have this gnawing feeling that faith and belief can help solve problems in all areas of our lives. If we only ask. Today I do a lot of tossing stuff in God's Hands and then forget about it due to my faith and belief in that prayer process.

COMPASSION FROM OTHERS

Due to all the surgeries for bone and skin injuries, I found myself having to live in a rehab center to recover for four months. The location of the broken bones made me unable to move on my own with crutches and so I had to be transferred by nursing assistants from bed to wheel chair. And without going into detail I had to live for a bit of time as a baby… if you catch my drift! It was in rehab I spent a lot of time going from basically lying in bed with many casts and finally therapy to get me to walk with a walker. You must get to a good walker stage before any thoughts of going home. On a happy note here, I am now walking without any assistance. It was the compassion, patience and encouragement of some great therapists and nursing staff hat made this happen.

There were many trying times due to medications and diet changes, but it was during this time I discovered the compassion of the nurses and to a greater extent, the certified nursing assistants. Those assistants made it much easier for me to endure these daily physical insults because of their compassion. You could spot those who truly cared for the patients and did not mindlessly perform tasks. I truly believe these nursing assistants are not paid high enough for the duties they perform . There was one lovely woman aide that worked the night shift quite a bit. Whenever I would thank her for the tasks she had to perform during my extreme times, she would smile and always say to me, "It was my pleasure to help". To this day I remember every act of kindness by the aides and how a few went over and above with their time, energy and hugs to stifle a worry and many tears.

Was this yet another string of compassion being bestowed by God to put the right people on my path during this part of the journey? Was it a lesson on compassion I needed to learn? Yes, I believe it was His compassion to lighten my load putting the right people on my path, but it also was to allow me to see goodness and compassion of others and how it made the world a better place. I was shown how compassionate people can make a shift. The atmosphere would change in the rehab center as we experienced someone going over and above with a great attitude and making the patients happy; just as we would see the change in the environment when an assistant was a slacker or mean spirited. Aides filled with compassion meant many happy patients.

The showing of compassion or love for another person shifts the life of both the giver and the receiver. The givers feel good by doing good and the receivers are uplifted. Sometimes that uplifting makes the receivers want to do more for someone else somewhat like paying it forward. Ever have that situation at a coffee shop when the person in front of you buys your coffee and you end up beaming away over it? Later that day you will find yourself still beaming and doing an act of kindness for someone else.

Strong compassion was on display daily at the therapy room during rehab, not only from the therapists but from the fellow wounded trying to get back their lives . Those fellow warriors were the best cheering section ever for encouragement when they viewed someone's accomplishment. They could have ignored and been absorbed in themselves, but they would go out of their way to show compassion for someone just trying to put one foot in front of the other.

I might mention here I am still experiencing compassion from family, friends and neighbors after I was able to do home recovery. My brother has become my biggest Angel these days. Travelling a great distance to do weekly shopping trips or taking me to appointments. I might add that the sibling sense of humor between us has been rediscovered too. My sister-in-law has made some tasty packaged meals even when she was going through her own injury. Oh lets also mention here all the baked goodies and plants for every occasion, or lack of occasion, from my dear neighbors. I think God has been keeping the compassion train going by whispering in a few ears.

A NEW LIFE BEGINS....

LEARNING COMPASSION AND LOVE FOR MYSELF

So I have learned the compassion of God toward His children, and have learned the compassion to and from others during recovery. But it was the months of home confinement healing the bones and wounds and doing things on my own that I also learned to experience compassion and love toward myself. I had days ahead of me existing without the hustle and noise of my own business which normally carried me through a day. There were times of television, computer, writing projects, therapy work, and assorted reading, but mostly there was a lot of time for reflection. I had the occasional visitor or running into a neighbor in the condo hallways when picking up the mail. There were a few outside doctor office visits. It was the height of an extreme flu season and we felt best to stay away from people as much as possible. Friend visits were on hold. Also, being winter and the ice and snow was not exactly a good combination for someone recuperating from bone breaks. The skin injury and subsequent skin grafting made it impossible to put boots on anyway. I had to wear backless mule type shoes during the healing.

So here I was living with a lot of quiet time. And it was in those quiet hours of meditation or just looking out the window at the winter scene that I felt closest to the spirit within. The voice within that wants your attention and wants to guide you but needs you to quiet down to hear. It was a time to reflect on the last few years of the hamster wheel way of my old life and what I truly wanted with the new. The injuries would put a few self-imposed restrictions on me in the new life too. I had fears I never had before to now deal with in that regard. I was being led to some self-discovery and getting more than a nudge to trust it.

Maybe God felt I needed that solitude to finally learn about what I truly loved and what would make me happy and whole. And a shocker, my business that I had once wrapped my whole existence around was not even on the list. If I didn't miss something from my life after it was gone, I definitely must have hung on way too long after the joy I once had passed. I lost my business the day of the accident yet never missed it during recovery. I missed the money not the business and all its wrappings.

So surprisingly during this down time, I did not rush to reopen the business. I preferred to let the injuries both physical and mental take all the time they needed to heal without any added burden.

In the beginning days of my business I think I was so thrilled with the challenge of building up the business. I enjoyed helping other business owners and did a damn good job at it. Through the years, due to the nature of the work, it wore me down. Yet I failed to see how that was hurting me. I guess the solitude made me aware of all the stress I had pushed aside. I began feeling my old business was not an avenue of joy for me. I was starting to wonder if I was even right for this type of work anymore. The more I stayed away from this business, the more I knew its time in my life was over. The voice within was showing me a new way forward. My soul was trying to tell me it is unthinkable that I trudge along out of obligation to clients or the fear of letting it go instead of living in joy. I should be spending my days doing something that would put the joy back in my daily life.

Was the accident allowed to happen as part of The Plan to change my life since I wasn't moving fast enough to help myself? After all, I didn't get any warnings not to take the walk that day, or stop somewhere along the way to avoid that driver. We all get those insights daily. So was it all allowed to happen but with great protection? I am not going to wrack my brain anymore on that issue. It's not for me to know now. But what I do know is that it is time to show compassion to myself and sprinkle the joy dust on me.

I had a few other miracles or discoveries that came along too during recovery, so I don't think closing that business was the sole reason.

One such issue was walking. It was in my quiet hours when I pined to go outside and just take a normal walk that I realized that too had needed changing. I had made my old joy of walking into just errands and was not out there for the joy of the movement, the weather or nature. When healed I will make a date with myself to go out and walk just for the joy of walking with no strings attached. I had turned a joy into drudgery. Funny how I had made myself do just one more walking errand that fateful day. A bit of irony there. I guess God was right to shake my life up and I surely needed that shake up. Or shall we say wake up!

The healing process was moving me to think of the future. Just as my old business was out of the picture, my future walking breaks after all the healing restrictions are gone was not going to be a duty for a bunch of errands. I was certainly going to appreciate a walk outside again… for the joy of walking!

I had self-published a book of a whimsical story told in rhyme years back. I have a manuscript of the second book in rhyme done. I wanted a rhyme trilogy depicting characters at various stages in life. I have a manuscript of a business book done. I was starting to wonder why I was given insight to start and finish those book projects long before the accident. Better yet, why was I not listening to insight that strong? Had I let life get in the way? Oh, I got the message now! And now in recovery, here I am pouring my heart out in another book to relate this miracle. I could have digested the miracle and then kept it inside instead of being used as a vehicle to make others aware.

I believe I am now being led to take a step in another direction, but know now, yes know, that I will be protected along the way on a new journey. Just as I was protected when I was led to start my old business and how it all worked out. How could I not think of great protection down the line in a new endeavor after experiencing that great protection in the accident? I don't believe God dishes out a dose here and not a dose there. But the keyword for me as to that protection is the belief I will be guided.

God was trying to get me to show some compassion for myself and do what I love and probably always was meant for me to do. I think it started way back when I was sixteen years old when I found the books of this wonderful author, Frances Parkinson Keyes. She would go to live in a place in the world and then would whisk her readers away to that spot and weave her story in that area. I had thought what a fascinating life that could be. Oddly, it was also that age that I learned my talent to write poetry of rhyme. My school picked me to represent them in the National Anthology of High School Poems. It was a humorous poem called Wonders of a Smile. Then a professor in college in a creative writing class would read everything I wrote to the class and tried to encourage me to switch to a school of journalism. There were many signs, but I wasn't listening and let life get in the way.

When you love someone you want to do everything to make them happy. God also wants me to love myself and do things to make me happy and filled with joy. I believe now each day should be filled with love, joy and peace. I believe now if you don't have that, you must do something to seek that out for yourself and do it without fear. I was now believing I could push through the fear of letting go of the familiar and seeking the new because God has my back. My accident within that Divine Event brought me to realize that. I got more than a tap on the shoulder in enlightenment.

And, I also started to feel my home bound recovery was not a waste of time or imprisonment. I can remember I started to feel joyful once the decisions were being made for my new life, and the subsequent anticipation of the new journey. I deserved to treat myself with compassion and reach for joy again. This interruption of life was a gift!

ONE LAST LESSON OF COMPASSION I NEEDED TO LEARN

Due to all the pain, suffering and loss, I had to work on developing compassion for the young driver that hit me. It would surely lead me to forgiveness if I could see from another perspective. In the beginning I would curse him for his careless or distracted driving because of all the surgeries and procedures I experienced. The loss of money due to enormous hospital bills and his insurance company's tiny settlement check that would never leave me much after lien holders took their share. Why did I have to be in financial straits at this stage of my life? Oh and he just goes his merry way. But then I started to think he may not be so merry after all. He may be realizing what his error had done to my body and my life. I put myself in his shoes and I felt I would have been so distraught, so perhaps he was too. Also was God giving him something to learn from the wreckage? Was he too perhaps living a life on a hamster wheel causing him to have distractions in life on important issues? God didn't seem to put up a roadblock for him to avoid hitting me that day. Maybe he too had choices or nudges that he was ignoring and using his free will. He too may have needed lessons to learn that this accident provided. But I if I am to heal totally from the injuries and fears, I will have to extend compassion and forgiveness because he may be a victim of sorts too. I have to believe he is not callous. I do believe if I am hurting he is also hurting because we are all one and connected. So if I let my heart show compassion toward him and forgive, somehow that same God of Compassion that helped to save me, will make his heart feel it. It's a struggle and hard to let go but for true healing, it must be done.

FINAL THOUGHTS

As burdensome as life can be at times, I am now believing life is far more magical. After all, I was captured in a safe haven and given an opportunity to feel the peace there all through a traumatic event. I was honored to see that beautiful heavenly destination even though it was not going to be my journey that day. My first clue of being saved should have been that no passed loved ones were there to help with adjustment or guidance.

My thoughts in the hospital were that it was so comfortable, so close to Heaven in that holding pattern, and darn, I am now going to have to deal with this earth stuff. But as comfortable and peaceful as it was, even with the injuries and life defeats I was going to have to go through, there were many joys I experienced to make up for leaving that beautiful time and space of peace. Yes, even in the learning of life lessons, there can be joys in starting over as you accomplish new things and meet your challenges. There is joy in finding love if you take the time to look for it in everyone and all living things. In that regard, let me throw in a little humor here and say that my plants look even more beautiful these days! Now why is that? Is it because I finally have the time to show them more care and they are feeling that love? Don't laugh, they too are a living part of this Universe. If people can feel your love and attention, and pets can feel that too, well my plants, which are a living form of God's creation, must feel it too. And in return they are giving me so much joy with their health and beauty.

I realize now I was missing so much on that hamster wheel. Never thought I would say this but I am grateful for that accident, for whatever reason it came about or why I got that protection. I am grateful for that experience of connecting with God and His compassion that day. I guess I will never know all the answers until the day I finally get the go-ahead signal to journey up that path to that glorious heavenly destination. The doors will finally open and those who weren't there to greet me that accident day are now guiding me inside and I am asked to stay.

ACKNOWLEGEMENTS

It is with great pleasure that I relate my gratitude for a few of the special earth angels that helped me through this journey.

My brother, Frank and his wife, Carolyn, for making me feel safe and secure living through the obstacles;

Special mention to two of the nursing assistants at the rehabilitation enter, Nguwah and Maria. Special mention to three of my rehab center therapists Janice, Shannon and Randy. The home therapist, Mae, for her expertise and sunshine personality and for getting to walking alone stage.

Gratitude to a few of my neighbors for all their acts of kindness at hospital and later in home bound recovery – Maria, Delores, Jessica and Ita. All those plants, homemade meals, bread, delicious strudel and assorted pastries were the best medicine ever.

To Trudi, my lawyer's assistant, who was not only helpful but a joy to deal with.

To Judy Johnston, A Hand in Healing, one of my friends in Canada, for sending me free distance energy healing sessions and they miraculously helped.

To Leigh Grissom, a fellow writer, for her constant encouragement.

To all my other friends and acquaintances, even those on Facebook and Twitter, for their encouragement. Special mention to Joe, who helped at the drop of a hat, with varied issues.

To my editor, Andrea Warden, for taking on the challenge.

Love to all of you!

Printed in the United States
By Bookmasters